PIANO
VOCAL
GUITAR

BEST OF BOTH WORLDS CONCERT

ISBN 978-1-4234-4561-6

Disney characters and artwork
© Disney Enterprises, Inc.

**Walt Disney Music Company
Wonderland Music Company, Inc.**

DISTRIBUTED BY

**HAL•LEONARD®
CORPORATION**

7777 W. BLUEMOUND RD. P.O. BOX 13819 MILWAUKEE, WI 53213

Visit Hal Leonard Online at
www.halleonard.com

Miley Cyrus

ROCK STAR

Words and Music by JEANNIE LURIE,
ARIS ARCHONTIS and CHEN NEEMAN

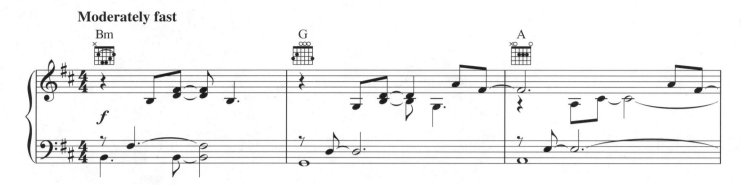

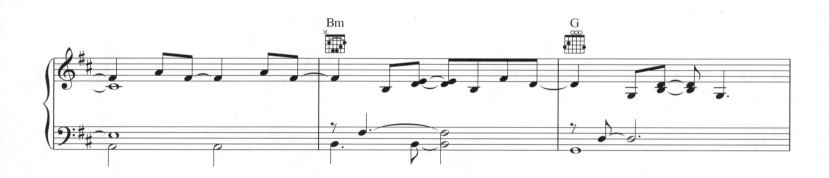

LIFE'S WHAT YOU MAKE IT

Words and Music by MATTHEW GERRARD
and ROBBIE NEVIL

Moderately fast

Don't let no
Why let be sad,

small frus - tra - tion
bro - ken - heart - ed?

ev - er bring you down, __
There's so __ much to do, __

All you got-ta do is re - al - ize that it's un -der your con -trol,

so let the good times rock and __ roll. _____

(Spoken:) Come on, everybody!

Do, do, do, do it now.

JUST LIKE YOU

Words and Music by ANDREW DODD
and ADAM WATTS

Lyrics:

in an ex - tra - or - di - nar - y world. ___

___ Try - ing to live, ___ try - ing to learn, ___ try - ing to just ___

___ be who ___ I am. ___

Who ___ I am. ___ I got

NOBODY'S PERFECT

Words and Music by MATTHEW GERRARD
and ROBBIE NEVIL

* Recorded a whole step lower.

PUMPIN' UP THE PARTY

Words and Music by
JAMIE HOUSTON

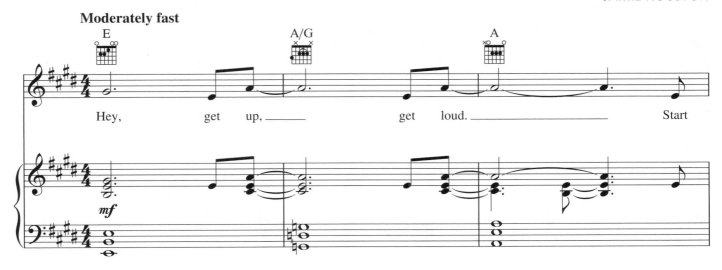

42

I GOT NERVE

Words and Music by JEANNIE LURIE,
KEN HAUPTMAN and ARUNA ABRAMS

WE GOT THE PARTY

Words and Music by
KARA DioGUARDI

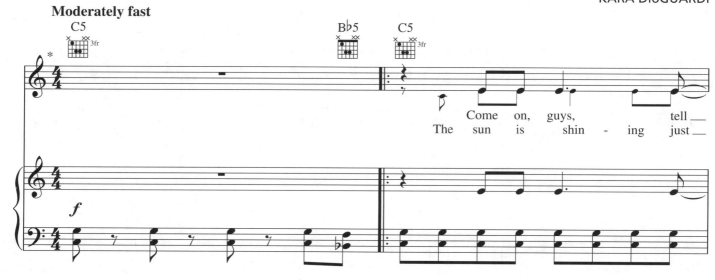

Come on, guys, tell
The sun is shin - ing just

me what we're do - ing.
the way we like it.

We're hang - in' 'round when we
Let's get out of this hall -

could be all o - ver the place.
way, show the world our face.

* Recorded a half step lower.

Turn this park _ in - to _ a club, _ the stars _ are lights _ _ and the moon _ is the vibe _ from a - bove. _ This skate - - board here's _ our ride, _ so pull _ on up; _ ev - 'ry - one _ is wait - - ing for us. _ An - y - where we are, an - y - where we go, ev - 'ry - bod - y

START ALL OVER

Words and Music by FEFE DOBSON,
SCOTT CUTLER and ANNE PREVIN

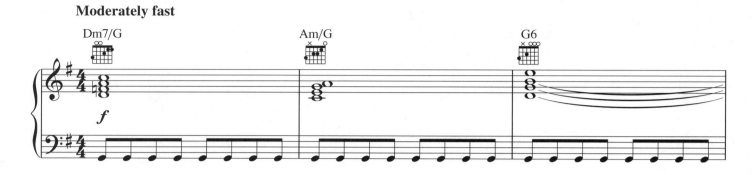

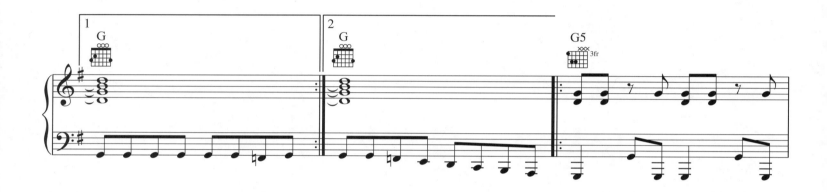

I have to won-der if _____ this wave's

Fan- tas- tic and _____ ro- man- tic, all _____

GOOD AND BROKEN

Words and Music by DESTINY HOPE CYRUS,
TIM JAMES and ANTONINA ARMATO

*Recorded a half step lower.

68

SEE YOU AGAIN

Words and Music by DESTINY HOPE CYRUS,
TIM JAMES and ANTONINA ARMATO

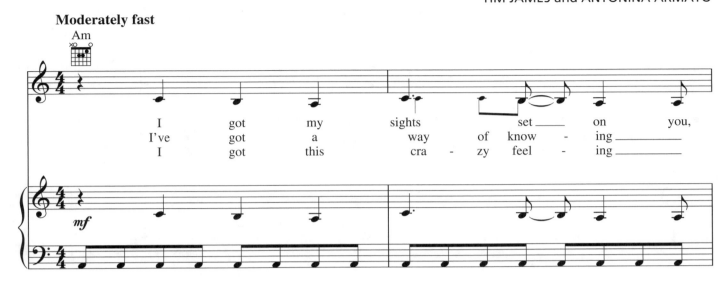

LET'S DANCE

Words and Music by DESTINY HOPE CYRUS,
TIM JAMES and ANTONINA ARMATO

Melody is written an octave higher than sung.

(Dance!)

When the night says hel - lo, yeah, get read - y to go. Turn it up, turn it loose, yeah, you've got _____ no ex - cuse. Just take _____

EAST NORTHUMBERLAND HIGH

Words and Music by SAMANTHA JO MOORE,
TIM JAMES and ANTONINA ARMATO

Just be-cause I liked you back then, ___

it does-n't mean I like ___ you now. ___

Just be-cause I liked you back then, ___ it does-n't mean I like you.

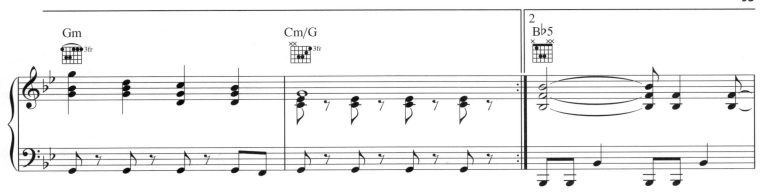

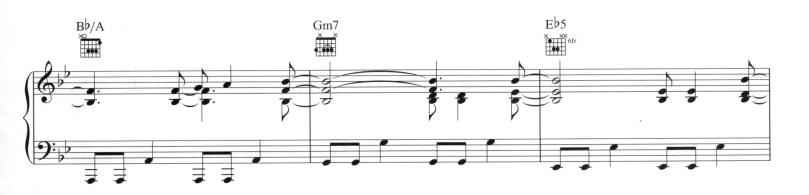

When you're stand - ing

G.N.O.
(Girl's Night Out)

Words and Music by MATTHEW WILDER
and TAMARA DUNN

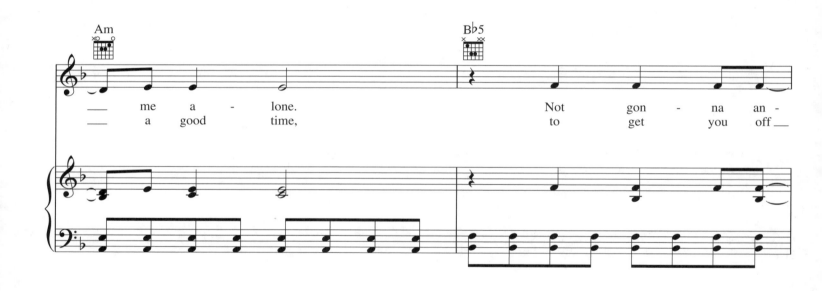

THE BEST OF BOTH WORLDS

Words and Music by MATTHEW GERRARD
and ROBBIE NEVIL

* Recorded a half step higher.

worlds. Chill it out, take it slow, ___ then you

rock out the show. You get the best of both ___

worlds. Mix it all to - geth - er and you

know that it's the best of both worlds.